WITHDRAWN

HOLIDAYS AROUND THE WORLD

Summer

June, July, and August

Cath Senker

Rourke
Publishing LLC

HOLIDAYS AROUND THE WORLD

Titles in this series:

Autumn

Spring

Summer

Winter

www.rourkepublishing.com

Picture Acknowledgments:
A1 *(title)*, 14; Paul Doyle 6; Eye Ubiquitous *(cover: bottom, right)*, 12; Sonia Halliday 9; Impact 15; Christine Osborne Pictures *(cover: top, centre; bottom, centre; top, left)*, 5, 7, 11, 19, 22, 24, 25, 26, 27, 28, 29; Panos 21 *(bottom)*; David Silverman *(cover: top, right)* 8; Topham Picturepoint 4, 10, 16, 17, 20, 21 *(top)*; Zul Muhkida *(cover: bottom, left)*, 13, 18, 23.

Title page photo: A group celebrates Midsummer's Day in Norway.

Note:
The quotations in this book are fictionalized accounts drawn from factual sources.

Library of Congress Cataloging-in-Publication Data
Senker, Cath.
Summer / Cath Senker.
p. cm. -- (Holidays around the world)
ISBN 1-59515-197-4 (hardcover)
1. Summer festivals. I. Title. II. Series.
GT4505.S46 2004
394.263--dc22
2004008011

Contents

Holidays in the Sun

Summer is a wonderful time for holidays. The weather is good, and everyone enjoys outdoor celebrations. Since ancient times, people across Europe have honored the power of the sun at midsummer. Many kinds of fruit, vegetables, and other crops ripen in the warm months. Jewish people celebrate this harvest at Shavuot (see pages 8–9).

The weather is hot and sunny in many countries during June, July, and August. In India, Hindus hold a spectacular outdoor festival called Ratha Yatra. The festival honors Krishna, whom many Hindus see as the Lord of the Universe. Hindus in other countries hold similar holidays.

A family enjoying a summer picnic with delicious fresh fruit

The magnificent Ratha Yatra festival in Puri, India. You can see all three chariots.

This book looks at holidays during the summer months in the **northern hemisphere**. Remember that on the other side of the world—in Australia and South America—it is winter then. And in **tropical** countries, such as the Caribbean islands, it can be hot all year round. Also, note that the Muslim holidays are not set according to the seasons. The Muslim holidays you will read about can take place at any time of the year.

Geeta's Ratha Yatra

"Every year, the Lord of the Universe and his brother and sister go on holiday. The images of the gods travel in amazing chariots, and everyone helps to carry them. I went to the temple dressed in my Indian clothes. We took turns pulling the chariot and sang beautiful *bhajans*—our hymns. My cousin in Puri in India says that thousands of people go to the procession there."
Geeta, Chicago, Illinois

The Martyrdom of Guru Arjan, JUNE

This Sikh festival is a *gurpurb*. *Gurpurbs* are special days to remember the births and deaths of the ten Sikh Gurus (teachers).

Guru Arjan, the fifth Guru, spent his life spreading the Sikh faith in India, about four hundred years ago. The Emperor of India accused him of writing bad things about Hindus and Muslims in the Sikh holy book. Guru Arjan said this was not true and refused to change the book.

The Guru was captured and tortured to death. He was pushed into boiling hot water and covered with baking hot sand. The poor Guru was not allowed to drink even a drop of water.

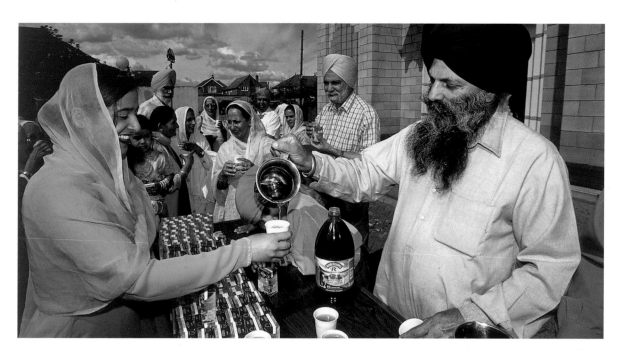

Sikhs hand out free cool drinks in memory of Guru Arjan.

6

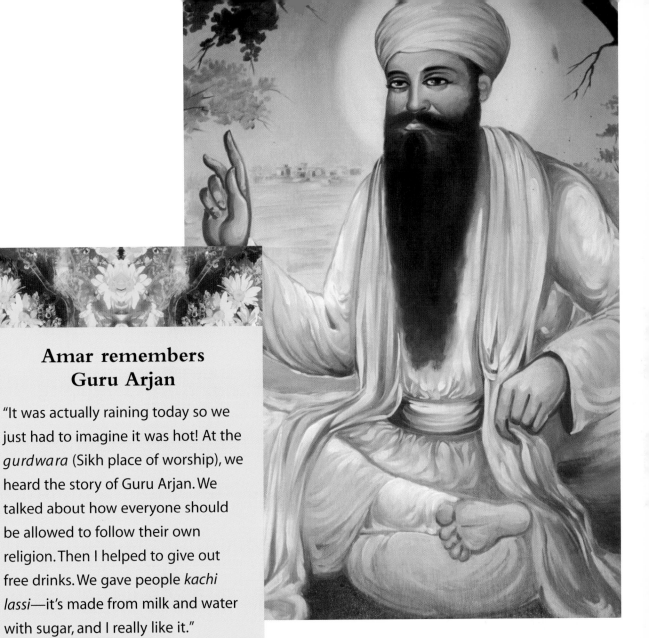

Amar remembers Guru Arjan

"It was actually raining today so we just had to imagine it was hot! At the *gurdwara* (Sikh place of worship), we heard the story of Guru Arjan. We talked about how everyone should be allowed to follow their own religion. Then I helped to give out free drinks. We gave people *kachi lassi*—it's made from milk and water with sugar, and I really like it."

Amar, London, England

An image of Guru Arjan. Many Sikhs have died for their religion.

At this *gurpurb*, Sikhs remember Guru Arjan by giving away cool drinks to people of all communities. They remember how the Guru stayed calm and cool throughout his terrible torture. It is hot in India at this time of year so people are very pleased to receive a refreshing cold drink. This friendly custom shows that Sikhs want to get along with people from different religions.

Shavuot, MAY OR JUNE

Shavuot is a joyful Jewish holiday that celebrates the wheat harvest. In Israel, this falls in the summer. Jewish people go out to the fields to sing and dance among decorated sheaves of wheat. Around the world, people decorate their **synagogues** with fresh summer flowers. They also bring fruit, just as in ancient times they brought the **first fruits** of the harvest as a gift to the Jewish temple.

Israeli children decorating baskets with flowers and wheat to celebrate Shavuot

Cheesecake is a popular dairy food at Shavuot.

Rachel's Shavuot

"At the synagogue, we listened to a talk about the Ten Commandments. They are rules for how to be good in life. Then it was party time! We'd decorated the place with flowers, and everyone had brought their favorite summer fruit—I brought apricots. My favorite Shavuot food is cheese-filled pancakes called *blintzes*. My grandma makes them. Her cheesecake is also good."

Rachel, Toronto, Canada

Shavuot is also the time when Jewish people remember how God gave them the *Torah*, their holy book. It includes the **Ten Commandments**. Some people stay up all night studying the *Torah* and praying.

A spread of delicious dairy foods is prepared for the holiday. Various stories explain the reason for the custom. It is said that when the Jews first received the *Torah* laws about how to prepare meat, they didn't quite understand them. So they ate dairy and other foods until they had worked them out. Another story says that the *Torah* is nourishing for the Jewish people just as milk is good food for a baby!

9

Pentecost, MAY OR JUNE

Pentecost falls at the same time as the Jewish festival of Shavuot. The Bible describes how Jesus' followers met 50 days after he had risen from the dead. Since Jesus' death, they had been scared to go out and tell people all about him. Now, they gathered together and were filled with the Holy Spirit—the power of God.

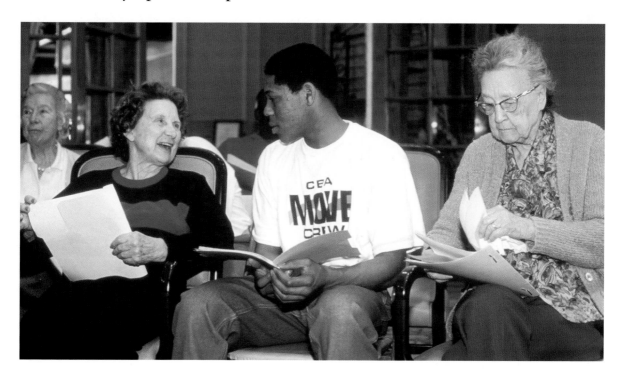

Helping other people is part of doing God's work in the world today.

Flames and a dove are symbols that represent the Holy Spirit. A dove represents the Holy Spirit's arrival. The first Christians described how it felt like flames on their head. The Holy Spirit gave them the power and the confidence to go out and spread Jesus' message in the world.

This was the beginning of the Christian Church. So Pentecost is the birthday of the Church. Christians celebrate their faith, which helps them continue God's work in the world today.

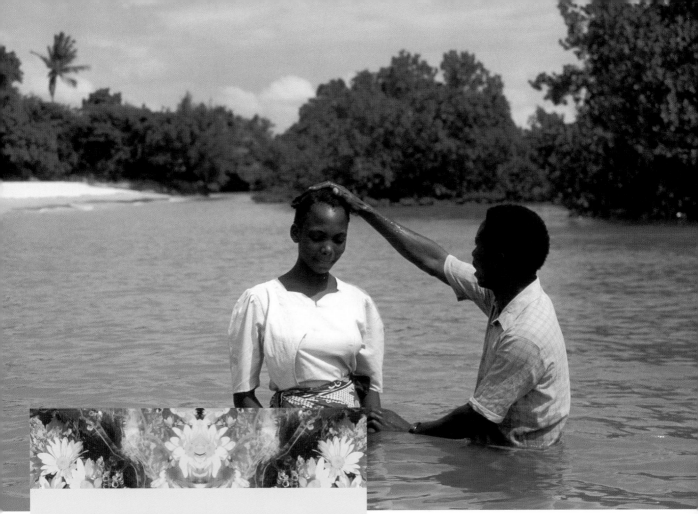

This woman has decided to become a Christian and is being baptized.

Lili's Pentecost

"At Pentecost we went to church and watched my friend's baby brother being baptized—he looked so sweet! Afterward, we went home and had a meal with some friends and lit candles to make it a special occasion. Mom and dad talked about when I was baptized as a baby. It means that I'm part of the Church family. Later, I filled a basin with water and baptized my doll."

Lili, The Hague, The Netherlands

Pentecost is a popular time for welcoming new people into the Church through **baptism**. During a special ceremony water is poured over the person. Most churches baptize babies. Some baptize older children and adults who have decided for themselves to join the Christian community.

Poson Day, JUNE

On Poson Day, Sri Lankan Buddhists celebrate the time when Buddhism came to their country. More than 2,000 years ago, Emperor Ashoka of India became a Buddhist. He was so enthusiastic about his new religion that he sent Buddhist teachers to other lands.

His son Prince Mahinda traveled to Mihintale in Sri Lanka. He told the King of Sri Lanka about Buddhism. The King became a Buddhist immediately and many men became followers. Women also wanted to become Buddhists. Emperor Ashoka sent his daughter, Princess Sanghamitta, to Sri Lanka, and she helped women join the religion.

The biggest Poson Day celebrations are in Mihintale. The weather is hot so the festival is held outdoors. There is a big procession, with giant floats carrying statues of people from the story of Prince Mahinda. Elephants wearing colorful coats surround the statues, and drummers accompany the procession.

Huge crowds attend the temple in Mihintale on this special day.

Hema's Poson Day

"Poson Day is my favorite festival. It gets really busy in Mihintale because thousands of people come to worship here. In the morning my family went to the temple and I joined in the *puja* (our worship). We heard a talk about Prince Mahinda. Later we joined the procession. It went really slowly through the streets, and the drummers set off fireworks—it was brilliant!"
Hema, Mihintale, Sri Lanka

Around the world, Sri Lankan Buddhists go to their temple on Poson Day. They listen to a talk and make **offerings** to the temple. It is an important time to be generous.

Making an offering of beautiful flowers at a shrine in Sri Lanka

Midsummer's Day, JUNE 21

In the northern hemisphere, Midsummer's Day on June 21 is the day with the most hours of daylight. Summer celebrations are held all across Europe. In the northern countries, people are delighted to enjoy some warmth after the long, cold winter. The farther north, the bigger the party!

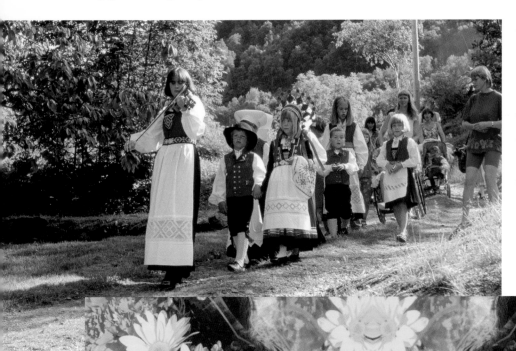

The midsummer festival in Utne, Norway. In Norway, it is traditional to light fires on Midsummer Eve.

Karl's Midsummer's Eve

"Last night was Midsummer's Eve. My friend and I went around the village collecting fuel for the bonfire. In the evening, my older brother's friends cut down a fir tree. The girls decorated it with **wreaths** of leaves and red ribbons. It was lighted up, and the men quickly collected the wreaths. The young men and women looked at each other through the wreaths to see who they might marry!"
Karl, Hamburg, Germany

The midsummer holiday comes from ancient customs. Many ancient stone circles and **monuments**, such as Stonehenge, were built so that the sun would rise over them in a certain way on Midsummer's Day. The holiday was later adopted by Christians; June 23 was named as St. John the Baptist Day.

The celebrations revolve around fire and water. In Estonia and Finland, the parties last a whole week. Everyone dances and sings around a bonfire. In Poland, the girls wear wreaths of flowers on their heads. Then they take off their wreaths, place a lighted candle on them, and let them float down the river.

Midsummer is celebrated in North Africa too. In Algeria and Morocco, people light bonfires. The bonfire smoke is supposed to have magical properties. It to said to cure the sick, get rid of bad luck, and even stop people's hair from falling out!

People dancing around the Stonehenge monument in England at Midsummer

Days to Remember,

June and July

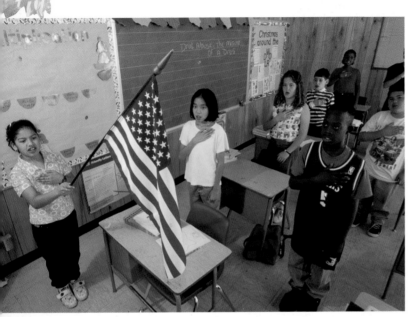

Schoolchildren show loyalty to their flag every day at school.

Flag Day

June 14 is National Flag Day. Flag Day was first celebrated in 1877, one hundred years after the United States adopted the Stars and Stripes. But the day was not made a **national holiday** until 1949, when President Harry Truman introduced it. Ever since then, Americans have been encouraged to display the Stars and Stripes outside their homes and businesses on June 14.

Independence Day

Each year, July 4 is celebrated as the day when the United States broke away from British rule in 1776. From that time forward, the United States has been an independent country. Americans celebrate in style, with parades, picnics, and fireworks.

The parades begin in the morning. Across the country, local baseball teams, school bands, and **baton twirlers** march through their town. People gather in the streets to watch, munching popcorn and waving flags.

Then it is time for a picnic or barbecue. Some families get together at home, but many people head outdoors, to the beach or to a lake. In the evening, there are fireworks displays in most American cities.

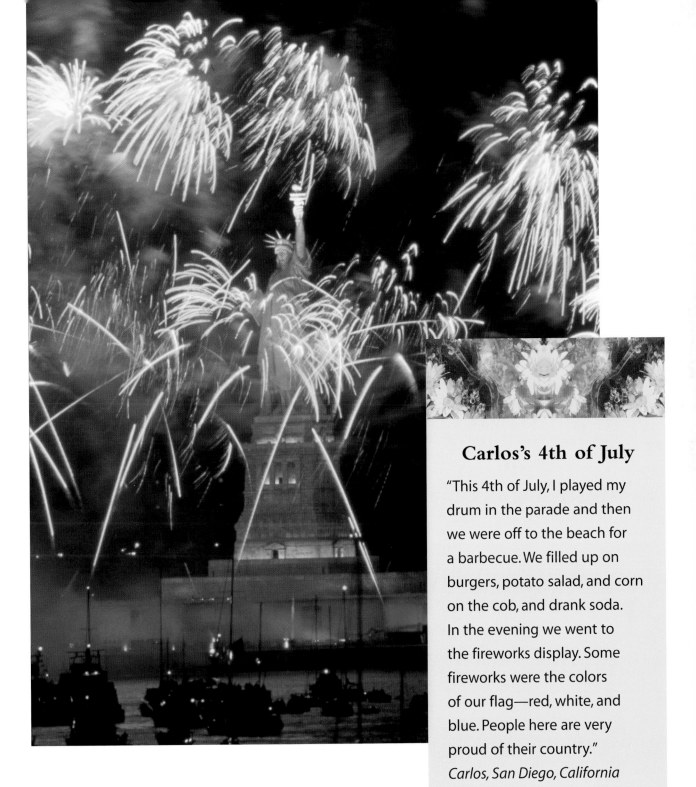

Carlos's 4th of July

"This 4th of July, I played my drum in the parade and then we were off to the beach for a barbecue. We filled up on burgers, potato salad, and corn on the cob, and drank soda. In the evening we went to the fireworks display. Some fireworks were the colors of our flag—red, white, and blue. People here are very proud of their country."
Carlos, San Diego, California

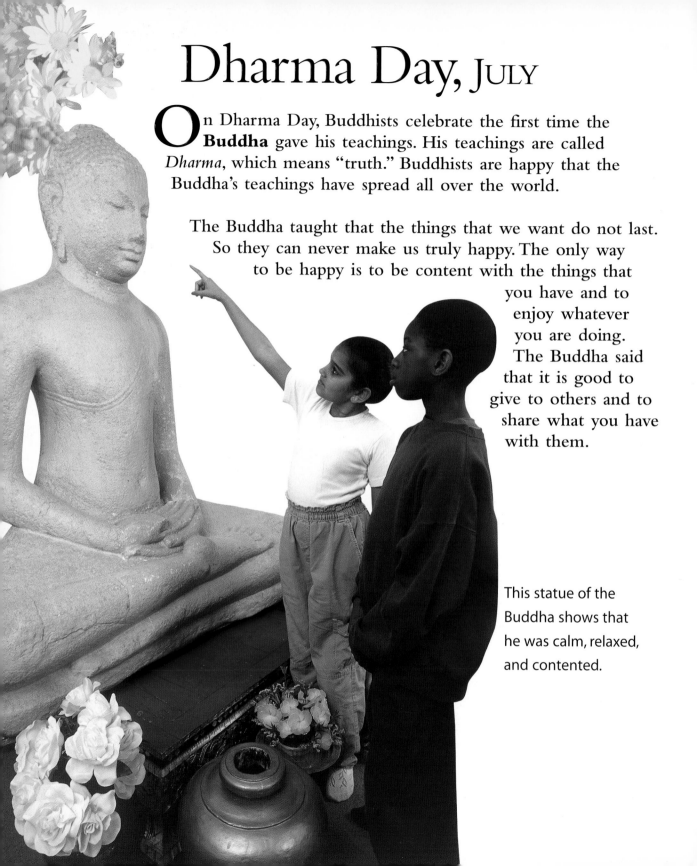

Dharma Day, JULY

O n Dharma Day, Buddhists celebrate the first time the **Buddha** gave his teachings. His teachings are called *Dharma*, which means "truth." Buddhists are happy that the Buddha's teachings have spread all over the world.

The Buddha taught that the things that we want do not last. So they can never make us truly happy. The only way to be happy is to be content with the things that you have and to enjoy whatever you are doing. The Buddha said that it is good to give to others and to share what you have with them.

This statue of the Buddha shows that he was calm, relaxed, and contented.

Sonia's Dharma Day

"On Dharma Day we heard about the Tibetan saint, Milarepa. His Guru tested his faith. He made him build, knock down, and rebuild a platform many times. Milarepa got really fed up until he understood he was being tested. He realized that he should keep his faith even during difficult times. Then we talked about how we can learn from tricky situations. I enjoyed spending time with my Buddhist friends on Dharma Day."
Sonia, Sydney, Australia

On Dharma Day, people go to the temple to listen to the Buddha's teachings from the holy book, the *Pali Canon*. Often a Buddhist teacher will read a story from the *Pali Canon* with the children and then discuss it. People take part in *puja* (worship), and they meditate. To meditate, they sit quietly with their thoughts. It helps them to become calm, happy, and wise. People bring **vegetarian** food to share afterward.

A young monk in Burma is studying the *Pali Canon*.

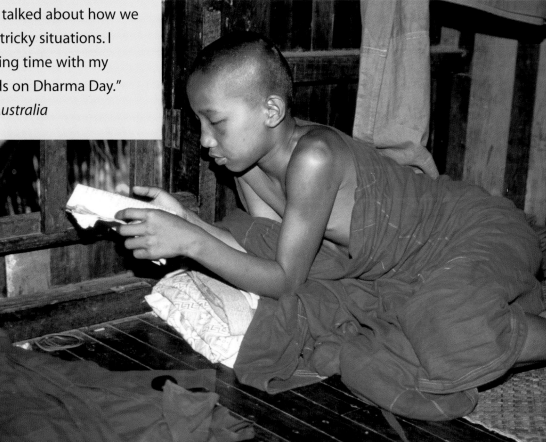

The Birth of Haile Selassie, July 23

All over the world, Rastafarians celebrate the birth of Ras Tafari. Ras Tafari became Emperor of Ethiopia in Africa in 1930. He took the name Emperor Haile Selassie.

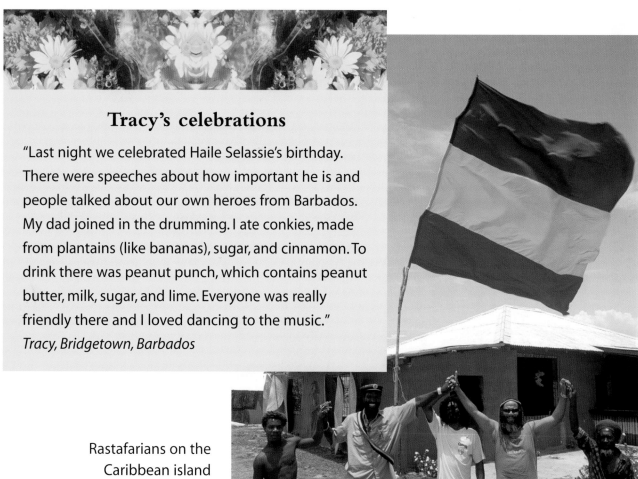

Tracy's celebrations

"Last night we celebrated Haile Selassie's birthday. There were speeches about how important he is and people talked about our own heroes from Barbados. My dad joined in the drumming. I ate conkies, made from plantains (like bananas), sugar, and cinnamon. To drink there was peanut punch, which contains peanut butter, milk, sugar, and lime. Everyone was really friendly there and I loved dancing to the music."

Tracy, Bridgetown, Barbados

Rastafarians on the Caribbean island of Jamaica joyfully waving the Rastafarian flag, which has the colors of the Ethiopian flag

Rastafarians believe that Haile Selassie was a god in human form. They believe he was important because he stood up for black people. Black people suffered because long ago they were taken away from Africa as slaves and treated badly. Even today, many black people are treated unfairly. Rastafarians believe that black people will be saved by returning to their first home, Africa.

Inset: Emperor Haile Selassie. Above: People in Jamaica dance to the sounds of reggae.

Today, Haile Selassie's birthday celebrations are biggest in the Caribbean islands, where the faith began. The climate is tropical and the weather is hot. Rastafarians come to gatherings and concerts. Many wear the colors of the Ethiopian flag—yellow, red, green, and black. The atmosphere is relaxed. There is Rastafarian drumming and chanting, and people dance to **reggae**. Often there are exhibitions of African art, and delicious vegetarian food is served.

Raksha Bandhan,

JULY OR AUGUST

Here is the story behind this Hindu festival. Once, the wicked demon-king Bali fought a god called Indra. Bali drove Indra out. Indra's wife, Sachi, was deeply upset. She went to ask the god Vishnu for help. He gave her a bracelet, made from threads, to tie around Indra's wrist. Indra fought another battle with Bali. This time, Indra defeated the demon-king because of the luck and protection offered by the bracelet. He won back his kingdom.

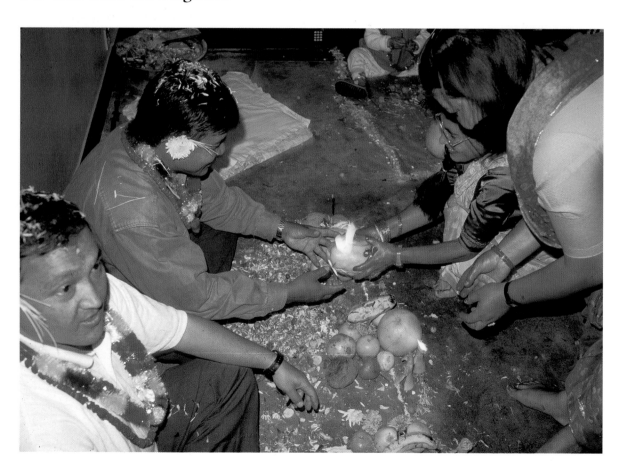

Sisters in Nepal making offerings to their brother on the occasion of Raksha Bandhan

Kunj's Raksha Bandhan

"Mom told me that *raksha* means 'protection' and *bandhan* means 'to tie.' At this holiday, all brothers and sisters—grown-ups too—show how much they love each other. I haven't got a sister so my cousin Nina gave me a *rakhi*. It's supposed to bring good luck and protection like in the story. In return, I gave Nina some money and she chose a pair of earrings.'"
Kunj, Gujarat, India

Raksha Bandhan is a holiday that helps families feel closer. In northern India, it also marks the start of the farming year.

First, the sister makes a mark on her brother's forehead with *kum-kum* paste, made from a red powder. She places some grains of rice on the mark. Next, she ties a *rakhi* (thread bracelet) around her brother's wrist and puts a candy called *barfi* in his mouth. She says a little prayer for God to look after him. In return, the brother promises to protect his sister from harm, and he offers her a present.

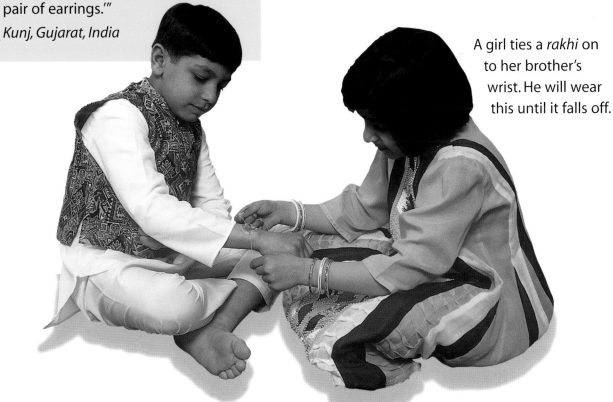

A girl ties a *rakhi* on to her brother's wrist. He will wear this until it falls off.

Krishna Janmashtami,
AUGUST OR SEPTEMBER

At this joyful festival, Hindus celebrate Krishna's birth. Krishna is one of the forms of God, and he is very special to many Hindus.

Because it is an important festival, Hindus **fast** during the day. In the evening, people gather at the *mandir*, the Hindu temple. It is believed that Krishna was born at midnight, so they wait eagerly for the moment. Everybody sings *bhajans* (hymns) about Krishna, and there is also dancing. As midnight approaches, there is an atmosphere of great excitement and joy.

Meera's Krishna Janmashtami

"On Krishna's birthday we went to the *mandir*. People were singing and playing Indian musical instruments. I played the *tabla*—a small drum. At midnight, all the kids took turns rocking Krishna's cradle, and we offered dishes of candy to him. He looked really cute! By this time, we were very hungry. We ate rice, **dhal**, and vegetables, and later we also got to eat Krishna's candies."

Meera, Kampala, Uganda

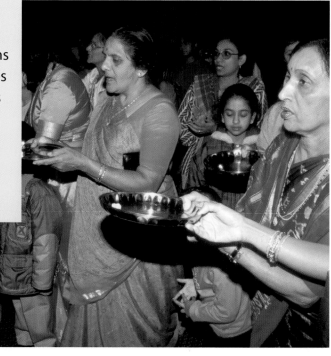

Worshippers at the temple, each holding a little tray with a candle for the *arti* ceremony held at midnight

24

An image of baby Krishna on display for his birthday in Singapore. He is being rocked like a real baby!

In the *mandir*, there is an image of baby Krishna in a cradle. At midnight, everyone gathers around the cradle for the *arti* ceremony. This involves moving lamps in circles in front of baby Krishna. People ring bells and blow a **conch shell** to announce the happy arrival.

In some places, fruit and candies are shared after midnight. In others, there's an Indian meal with rice and vegetables. Many Hindus eat tasty dishes made with milk and butter because it is said that Krishna loved dairy foods.

The *Guru Granth Sahib,*

SEPTEMBER

Sikhs gather at this holiday to celebrate their holy book, the *Guru Granth Sahib*. It contains hymns called *shabads*, which were written by the Sikh Gurus—and also by Hindu and Muslim holy men. The *shabads* are written in a language called Gurmukhi, the written form of the Indian language, Punjabi. They are poems that can be sung to music. Music is extremely important in Sikh worship.

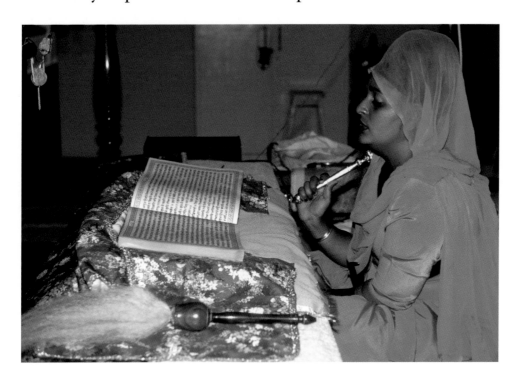

Both men and women may read from the *Guru Granth Sahib*.

In 1708, the tenth Guru, Guru Gobind Singh, announced that he was the last human Guru. From then on, Sikhs were to use the *Guru Granth Sahib* as their guide. They show great respect to their holy book, honoring it just like the human Gurus.

As Sikhs enter the *gurdwara*, they bow and pray to the Guru Granth Sahib. When it is not being read, it is covered and kept in a special place in the *gurdwara*.

At the ceremony, people come to the *gurdwara* to worship. They think about how best to follow the teachings of their holy book.

Young people learn Gurmukhi so they can read their holy book.

Kiran's celebrations

"Two days before the festival, my mother went to the *gurdwara* to help read our holy book. The reading of the whole book is called *Akhand Path* and it takes 48 hours! We do it at all the holidays. On the day, we sang hymns and listened to a talk about why our holy book is important. Afterward we had our shared meal, called *langar*. I had two portions of *kheer* for dessert."

Kiran, Mombasa, Kenya

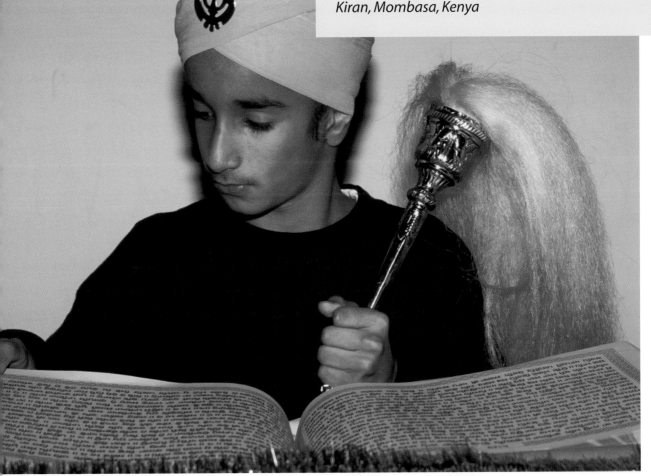

Lailat ul-Miraj

On this night, Muslims celebrate the **Prophet Muhammad's** extraordinary journey through the heavens. When the Prophet Muhammad was about 50, he was having a terrible time. It had been ten years since he received the message from **Allah** to go out and preach about the one true God. But few believed him. People laughed at him, and he was treated badly.

It is said that one night the angel Jibril (Gabriel) shook Muhammad awake and took him to Jerusalem on a winged animal called *al-Buraq* (the lightning). He was taken up through the seven heavens, where he met all the earlier Jewish prophets—also honored by Muslims. He rose to Allah's presence, a place of great peace and pure light. Here it was decided that Muslims should pray five times a day.

It is said that Muhammad rose to heaven from a rock that lies inside the stunning Dome of the Rock mosque in Jerusalem.

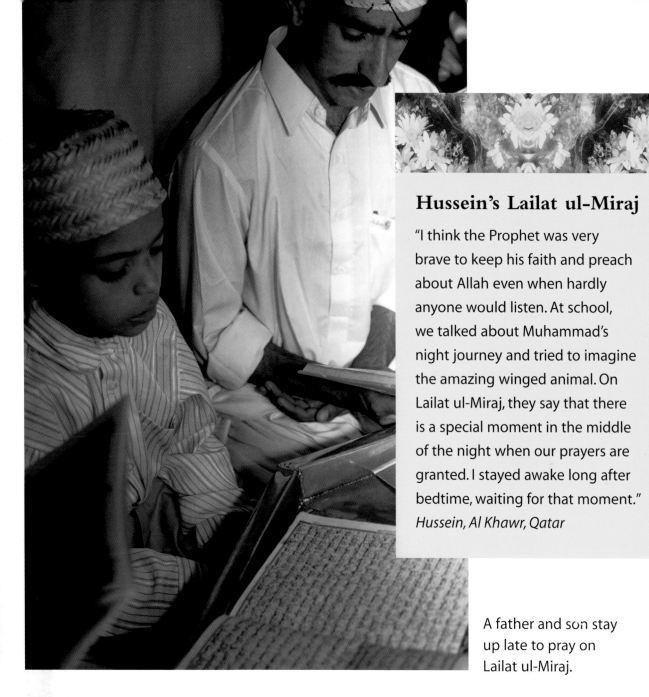

Hussein's Lailat ul-Miraj

"I think the Prophet was very brave to keep his faith and preach about Allah even when hardly anyone would listen. At school, we talked about Muhammad's night journey and tried to imagine the amazing winged animal. On Lailat ul-Miraj, they say that there is a special moment in the middle of the night when our prayers are granted. I stayed awake long after bedtime, waiting for that moment."
Hussein, Al Khawr, Qatar

A father and son stay up late to pray on Lailat ul-Miraj.

The night journey to the heavens gave Muhammad great strength at a difficult time in his life.

On Lailat ul-Miraj, some people stay up all night praying. Children practice saying their prayers and learn about the meaning of Muhammad's night journey.

Calendar of Holidays

Most religions follow a lunar calendar, based on the moon's movements, rather than a solar calendar. They adjust the calendar to keep the festivals in their season. Muslims don't adjust their calendar, so the festivals can be at any time of the year and are not related to the seasons. Sikh festivals are usually three days long because they include the two-day reading of the Sikh holy book before the festival day.

2004

Pentecost	May 30
Poson Day	June 9
Shavuot	June 13–14
Flag Day	June 14
The Martyrdom of Guru Arjan	June 16
Midsummer's Day	June 21
Independence Day	July 4
Dharma Day	July 15
The Birth of Haile Selassie	July 23
Raksha Bandhan	August 30
The Guru Granth Sahib	September 1
Krishna Janmashtami	September 6
Lailat ul-Miraj	September 12

2005

Pentecost	May 15
Poson Day	June 9
Shavuot	June 13–14
Flag Day	June 14
The Martyrdom of Guru Arjan	June 16
Midsummer's Day	June 21
Independence Day	July 4
Dharma Day	July 15
The Birth of Haile Selassie	July 23
Raksha Bandhan	August 19
Krishna Janmashtami	August 27
The Guru Granth Sahib	September 1
Lailat ul-Miraj	September 1

2006

Shavuot	June 2–3
Pentecost	June 4
Poson Day	June 9
Flag Day	June 14
The Martyrdom of Guru Arjan	June 16
Midsummer's Day	June 21
Independence Day	July 4
Dharma Day	July 15
The Birth of Haile Selassie	July 23
Raksha Bandhan	August 9
Krishna Janmashtami	August 16
Lailat ul-Miraj	August 22
The Guru Granth Sahib	September 1

Glossary

Allah (AHL uh) The Muslim name for God.

baptism (BAP tiz um) A Christian ceremony. Water is poured on to a person to welcome him or her to the Church.

baton twirlers (buh TAWN TWERL urz) People who march with a band, holding a long stick that they throw in the air in a special way.

Buddha (BOOD uh) The man who started the Buddhist religion.

conch shell (CONK SHELL) The outer shell of a sea creature called a conch.

dhal (DAHL) A dish made with lentils.

fast To go without food or without certain foods. Some Hindus even go without water on the day of Krishna Janmashtami.

first fruits (FURST FROOTZ) The first produce of the season, often offered to God.

gurdwara (GOOD wah ruh) The building where Sikhs go to meet and worship.

Guru (guh ROO) A holy Buddhist or Sikh teacher.

kheer (KEER) An Indian dessert made with rice, milk, and sugar.

monuments (MON yuh mentz) Ancient buildings that were made to celebrate something, such as the sun at midsummer.

national holiday (NASH uh nel HOL uh day) An important day that is a holiday in the whole country.

northern hemisphere (NOR thern HEM uh sfeer) The northern half of the Earth. The southern half of the Earth is called the southern hemisphere.

offerings (OFF uh ringz) Food, flowers, or other gifts that are placed in front of statues of the Buddha to give thanks for his teachings.

Prophet Muhammad (PROF et MOO ham ed) Muslims believe that Muhammad was the last prophet to bring Allah's message to the world.

reggae (REGG ee) Popular music with a strong beat.

synagogues (SIN uh GOGS) Buildings where Jewish people meet and worship.

Ten Commandments (TEN kum MAND mentz) The most important rules for Jewish people about how to live and worship. It is believed that they were given by God to the Jewish people.

tropical (TRAHP uh kul) Countries that are tropical are in the tropics, the hottest area of the world. This area is just above and just below the equator, an imaginary line drawn around the middle of the Earth.

vegetarian (VEJ uh ter ee en) A type of food that contains no meat or fish, or a person who does not eat meat or fish.

wreaths (REETHS) Circles of flowers or leaves.

Further Reading

Breuilly, Elizabeth et al. *Festivals of the World: The Illustrated Guide to Celebrations, Customs, Events and Holidays.* Facts on File, 2002

Cooper, Ilene. *Jewish Holidays All Year Round.* Abrams, 2002

Ganeri, Anita. *Christian Festivals Throughout the Year.* Smart Apple Media, 2003

Ganeri, Anita. *Hindu Festivals Throughout the Year.* Smart Apple Media, 2003

Landau, Elaine. *Independence Day: Birthday of the United States.* Enslow, 2001

Senker, Cath. *My Buddhist Year.* Hodder and Stoughton, 2003

Senker, Cath. *My Muslim Year.* Hodder and Stoughton, 2003

Websites to Visit

www.amaana.org/islam/muslimholidays.htm
www.urbandharma.org/udharma3/holidays.html
www.melizo.com/festivals/
www.aish.com/holidays/
www.holidays.net/independence

Index

All numbers in **bold** refer to pictures.